**Community Helpers**

# TV Reporters

by Tracey Boraas

**Consultant:**
John Sears
News Director, KPTV
Portland, Oregon

**Bridgestone Books**
an imprint of Capstone Press
Mankato, Minnesota

Bridgestone Books are published by Capstone Press
818 North Willow Street, Mankato, Minnesota 56001
http://www.capstone-press.com

*Library of Congress Cataloging-in-Publication Data*
Boraas, Tracey.
   TV reporters/by Tracey Boraas
   p. cm.—(Community helpers)
   Includes bibliographical references and index.
   Summary: An introduction to TV reporters, their work, dress, tools, schooling, and
importance in the community.
   ISBN 0-7368-0075-1
   1. Television broadcasting of news—United States—Juvenile literature. I Title. II. Series:
Community Helpers (Mankato, Minn.)
PN4888.T4B67 1999
070'.92'273—dc21                                      96-16804
                                                                          CIP
                                                                          AC

**Editorial Credits**
Michael Fallon, editor; James Franklin, cover designer; Sheri Gosewisch, photo researcher

**Photo Credits**
Frances M. Roberts, 6, 18
Frank S. Balthis, 10
James L. Shaffer, cover
Leslie O'Shaughnessy, 8
Michael Worthy, 4
Photo Network, Eric R. Berndt, 20
Unicorn Stock Photos/Aneal Vohra, 12; Florent Flipper, 14
Visuals Unlimited, 16

# Table of Contents

## TV Reporters

TV reporters appear on TV. They report
the news. TV reporters tell stories about
events in communities. They talk about
how events affect people.

5

## What TV Reporters Do

TV reporters interview people in the communities where events happen. They ask people questions to understand what happened. TV reporters write stories based on what they learn. They tell their stories on TV news shows.

## Where TV Reporters Work

TV reporters go to many places to report on events. They may go to schools, hospitals, or government buildings. They may report on fires or storms. Reporters tell stories from the places where events happen. They also report on events from TV stations.

## Kinds of TV Reporters

TV reporters report many kinds of news events. Some TV reporters talk about the weather. Others report only on sports or government news. Some TV reporters travel around the world to report events.

## Tools TV Reporters Use

TV reporters use microphones when they talk to people. Microphones help to record what people say. TV reporters sometimes use cameras to tape events. They also use computers to write stories.

## TV Reporters and Vehicles

TV reporters sometimes use vehicles to travel to news events. News vans carry the equipment that reporters need. Reporters also may fly to events in helicopters. This kind of aircraft can take off and land in small spaces.

## TV Reporters and School

Many people go to college to become TV reporters. People study in colleges after they finish high school. College students study ways to interview people. They also learn how to write stories about events.

## People Who Help TV Reporters

News photographers use cameras to tape events for TV reporters. News writers sometimes help reporters gather facts and write stories. People in communities may call reporters with ideas for stories.

## How TV Reporters Help Others

TV reporters help people understand their communities and the world. TV reporters warn people about emergencies. They tell people how to stay safe during dangerous events.

# Hands on: Report an Interesting Story

Reporters work hard to report interesting stories. They ask people questions and write down the answers. You can see what it is like to be a reporter.

## What You Need

An even number of players
Pencils and paper

## What You Do

1. Have each player choose a partner. One partner should be the reporter. The other will answer the reporter's questions. Have the reporters write their partners' names at the top of the paper.
2. Have the reporters ask their partners some questions. They could ask if their partners have a hobby. Or they could ask about the most interesting places their partners have visited.
3. The reporters should write down their partners' answers on the paper.
4. Have the reporters take turns telling their partners' stories to the group.
5. Have the reporters trade places with their partners. Repeat steps 1 through 4.

## Words to Know

**helicopter** (HEL-uh-kop-tur)—an aircraft that can take off or land in small spaces

**interview** (IN-tur-vyoo)—to ask someone questions about something important

**microphone** (MYE-kruh-fone)—a tool that helps to record what people say

**news photographer** (NOOZ foh-TOG-raf-ur)—a person who uses a camera to record pictures of events

# Read More

**Duvall, Jill D.** *Mr. Duvall Reports the News.* Our Neighborhood. Danbury, Conn.: Children's Press, 1997.

**Miller, Marilyn F.** *Behind the Scenes at the TV News Studio.* Austin, Texas: Raintree Steck-Vaughn, 1996.

# Internet Sites

**Get Real! Story Archives**
http://www.wpt.org/getreal!/story/story.htm
**What's New**
http://www.cbc4kids.ca/regular/whats-new/default.html

# Index

J070
B
Boraas
TV reporters